All rights reserved. No part of this book may be reproduced, stored in a retrieval system or transmitted, in any form or by any means, mechanical, photocopying, recording or otherwise, without any prior written permission of the publisher.

© B. Jain Publishers (P) Ltd.

Published by Kuldeep Jain for
Pegasus
An imprint of
B. JAIN PUBLISHERS (P) LTD.
An ISO 9001 : 2000 Certified Company
1921/10, Chuna Mandi, Paharganj, New Delhi 110 055 (INDIA)
Tel.: +91-11-4567 1000   Fax: +91-11-4567 1010
Email: info@bjain.com   Website: **www.bjain.com**

Printed in India by
J.J. Offset Printers

PEGASUS ENCYCLOPEDIA LIBRARY

Sports
BASKETBALL

Edited by: Pallabi B. Tomar, Hitesh Iplani
Managing editor: Tapasi De
Designed by: Vijesh Chahal, Anil kumar
Illustrated by: Suman S. Roy, Tanoy Choudhury
Colouring done by: Vinay Kumar, Kiran Kumari & Pradeep Kumar

CONTENTS

What is basketball? 3

Basketball court 5

Equipment 9

The game 11

Rules 14

Players' positions 19

Scoring 20

Governing bodies 21

Major events 22

Other basketball games 23

Basketball legends 24

Test Your Memory 31

Index 32

What is basketball?

Basketball can be played both indoors and outdoors. In a basketball game, players attempt to throw a round air-filled ball (also called basketball) through a raised metal hoop and net. This apparatus functions as a goal for the playing teams. Two teams of five players each compete against each other on a specially made basketball court.

The team with more points at the end of the game is declared to be the winner. The ball is manoeuvred with hands and can be moved around in the court by bouncing (dribbling) or by passing it between fellow teammates.

The beginning

Unlike most of the sports, the story of invention of basketball is well documented and is very recent. It was invented by a Canadian physical education teacher Dr James Naismith in December 1891. Naismith thought of the game when the education department of the Young Men's Christian Association Training School (now Springfield College) asked him to find an energetic indoors sport for the school athletes to play during winters.

Astonishing fact

The first men's college basketball game was played between the University of Iowa and the University of Chicago on 18th January, 1896.

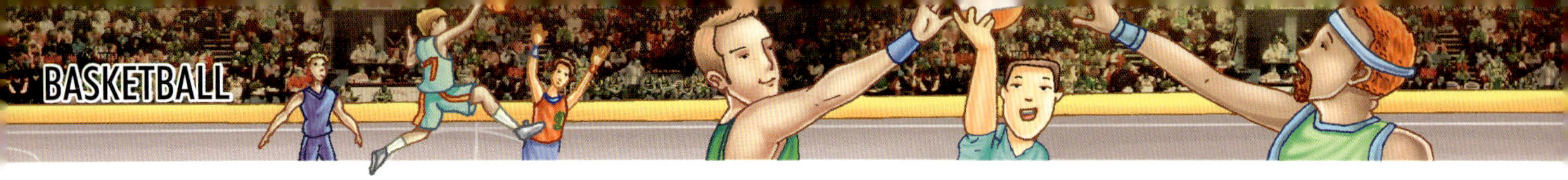

BASKETBALL

Dr Naismith combined elements of outdoor games like soccer and lacrosse (a game played with a solid rubber ball, and a racquet with a long handle) with a game he had played in childhood, Duck on a Rock. In Duck on a Rock, players try to hit a target placed on a height with stones. After Dr Naismith had written the basic rules he nailed a peach basket at a height of 3.05 m onto a balcony wall of a playing court.

The players were supposed to throw the ball into the basket. Since the basket was closed from the bottom someone had to climb on a ladder to bring down the ball each time someone managed to put the ball into the basket. Due to this inconvenience, the basket was replaced with a net hanging on a circular metal hoop. Later on, the bottom of the net was also removed so that the ball could fall through.

Another problem was the interference people sitting near the basket caused whenever the ball reached around the goal during the play. To check this, the hoop was joined to a backboard.

Astonishing fact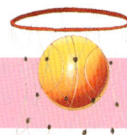

Originally, soccer ball was used to play basketball. A rough version of the modern basketball was invented in 1942.

Basketball court

Basketball is played on a specially designed basketball court. It is a rectangular floor with baskets at either end.

Surface

The surface of the basketball court used in professional matches, especially when played indoors, is usually made of hardwood, often maple. It is highly polished to allow smooth movement of the players. Suspended plastic interlocking tiles are also used as surface for indoor basketball courts.

For outdoor surfaces, blacktop, plastic interlocking tiles, asphalt or other similar materials are used.

Dimensions

The size of the basketball court varies according to the organisation the match is being played under. In a National Basketball Association match, the court is 28.65 m long and 15.24 m wide. International Basketball Federation (FIBA) prescribes the use of a slightly smaller court, measuring 28 m in length and 15 m in width. The use of smaller courts is allowed as long as they are at least 26 m long and 14 m wide. The baskets are always 3.05 m above the floor.

Astonishing fact

Some outdoor basketball courts are commonly called 'blacktop' referring to the asphalt surface used to make them.

BASKETBALL

Sections of a basketball court

A basketball court is divided into two equal halves by the **midcourt line**. The borders alongside the length of the court are called the **sidelines**. The lines at both the ends of the court that define the width of the court are called the **baselines** or the **endlines**.

Three-point line or the three-point arc

The three-point line extends around the basket in a near semicircle (like an arc), and its distance from the basket differs according to the level of play.

While a shot through the opponent's basket would result in two points to the team making the goal, a shot made from outside the three-point line would yield one extra point, that is, three points. However, the player making the three-pointer shot should have both of his feet behind the arc as he makes this shot. Once the ball is out of his hands either foot is allowed to land on the other side of the arc. If the shooting player steps on the three-point line, only two points will be awarded.

The distance from the centre of the circular metal rim of the basket to the three-point line varies according to the level of play or league. It has changed several times in the past.

Astonishing fact

The first person to hit a three point basket was Chris Ford on October 12, 1979.

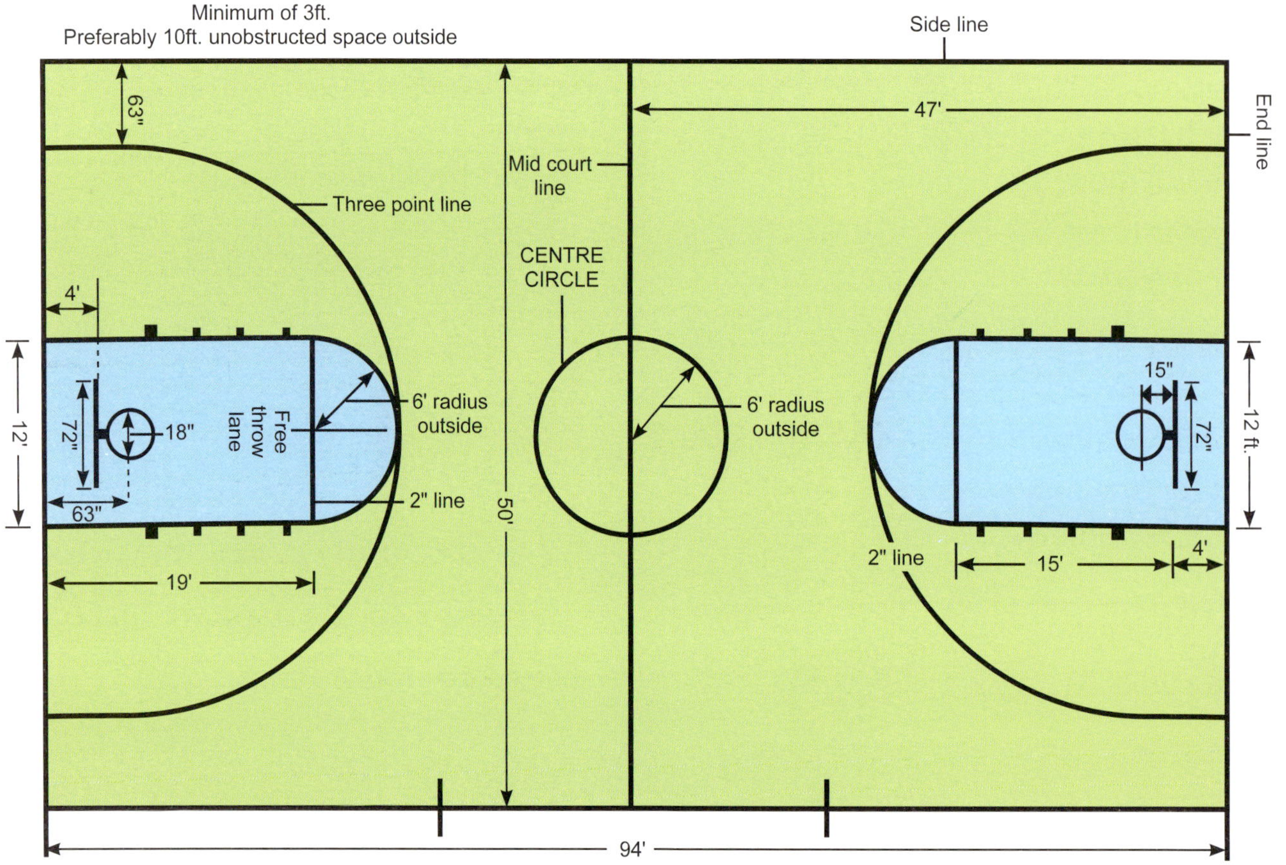

6

Centre circle

With the midpoint of the mid court line as the centre, a circle is drawn with a radius of 3.6 m. This is called the **centre circle**. This is where the game starts.

To start the game the referee throws the ball in the air standing in the centre circle. This is called the **centre toss**. Only two players from opposing teams are permitted to enter this area during the toss. Both the players have to jump and try to push the ball in the hands of a player of their own team. After the centre toss the centre circle becomes available for play to the rest of the team.

Free throw line

Free shots are granted to the player who has been fouled against by the player of the opposing team. These free shots are taken from the free throw line which is 4.57 m from the basket.

These shots are called free because nobody guards the shooter (the player who is making the shot) during the shot. One point is awarded to the team of the shooter if he scores a basket. However, while making a free throw the feet of the shooter must not cross the free throw line otherwise the shot will not be considered.

Astonishing fact

The only thing that has not changed since the day basketball was invented is the height of the hoop.

Free throw lane

During the free throw shot the rest of the players stand in a line alongside the free throw lane or behind the shooter. The free throw lane is a rectangular box 3.7 m to 4.9 m wide. Its length, as measured from the basket to the free throw line, is 4.6 m at all levels. Only four players can stand on either sides of the lane. They are not allowed to interfere with the free shot.

Key

The key (also known as the **shaded lane** or the **restricted area**) is the area including the free throw lane, the free throw line and the baselines. A circle with a radius of 1.8 m is drawn with the midpoint of the free throw line as the centre. It is also a part of the key. The purpose of the key is to prevent players from staying beneath the basket for long periods.

Perimeter

The area outside of the free throw lane and inside the three-point line (or the arc) is known as the perimeter. Shots made in this area are called **perimeter shots** or medium-range shots.

Low post area

The area that is outside the free throw lane but is closest to the basket is known as the **low post area**.

Astonishing fact

Before backboards were introduced, players used wall as support for climbing and scoring a goal.

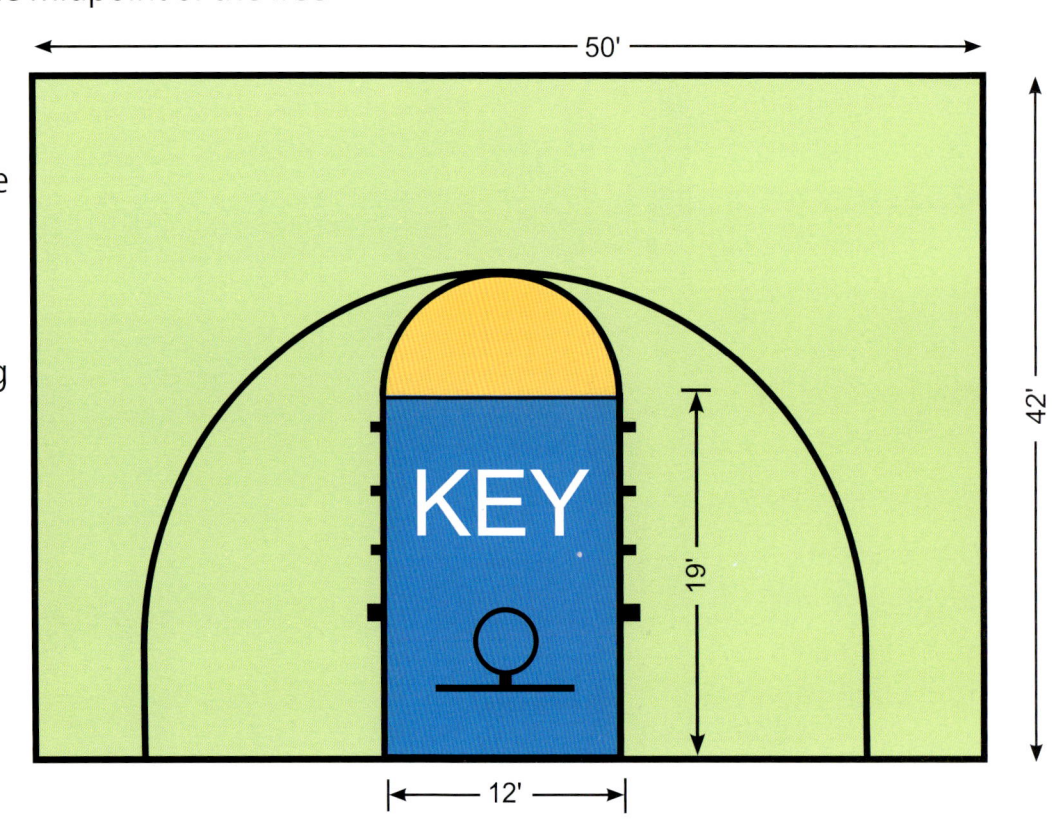

Equipment

The equipment used in a basketball game is quite minimal. The most important playing equipment is the basketball. Then, a hoop with a basket made of net is required. The basket, along with the hoop, gets attached to a backboard.

Basketball

A basketball is round in shape and its external covering is made of materials like leather, rubber or synthetic. The circumference of a basketball is between 75 cm to 78 cm. It weighs around 600 to 650 gm. The air pressure maintained in a basketball should be such that if it is dropped from a height of 1.8 m on to the surface of the court, it will rebound to a height of 1.2 m to 1.4 m.

Astonishing fact

The first basketball was brown in colour. In the late 1950s, Tony Hinkle for the first time introduced an orange coloured ball that was more visible to the players and the spectators.

The hoop

The ball gets shot into a circular hoop. This hoop is usually made of steel and is called a rim. The rim has a diameter of 18 inches. At all levels of competition, the rim is 3.06 m above the surface of the court and 121.9 cm inside the baseline.

Net

The net is attached to the rim by little hooks. Nets are usually made out of nylon or polyester. It measures 182.9 cm in length and 106.7 cm in width.

Backboard

The rim (or hoop) along with the net is then joined to the backboard. The backboard gives an extra advantage to the players by acting like a rebound surface for the ball, that is, the ball gets bounced back after hitting the backboard. It is usually made of glass, graphite or fibreglass. The backboard is usually 45.7 cm high and 61.0 cm wide.

Backstops

A backstop is used to hold the backboard in a fixed position above the ground. They can be mounted to a wall, free standing or can be suspended from a ceiling.

Other than these, the team hosting the match is usually responsible for providing a clock, a time-out watch, markers displaying the numbers 1 to 5 for use by the scorer to indicate how many fouls a player has committed, etc.

Player equipment

A basketball player's standard uniform consists of a pair of shorts and a jersey or a sleeveless vest. These enable smooth movement during the game. Players wear sneakers that provide extra ankle support.

Also, some other personal equipment like towels, mouthpieces, knee and elbow pads and eye or nose protection are also used by the players.

The game

Team members

Two five-player teams play against each other. Unlimited number of substitutions is available to both the teams. However, they can only be made when the play has been stopped. The coach of a team supervises the progress of his team and plans different strategies for them.

Each team is allowed up to five substitutes, who must stay off the court until the coach decides to replace an on-court player (known as making a substitution). Substitutions maybe made at time-outs, jump balls or when play is stopped for a foul.

The centre toss

The play starts in the centre circle. The game is started by the referee by tossing the ball up in air between two players from opposing teams. The players try to push the ball to their team mates. Once the ball is in the possession of one of the teams, the actual play starts. The players can now pass, throw, tap, roll or dribble the ball in any direction.

The objective

Each team has an assigned basket at each end of the court. The aim of the game is to throw the ball through the opponent's basket while stopping the other team from gaining the possession of the ball and scoring goals.

Astonishing fact

The first official basketball game played on January 20, 1892 had nine players on each side.

11

BASKETBALL

The team in possession of the ball is considered **offence** while the other team is considered **defence**. While playing offence, the object is to score a goal. The defence team, on the other hand tries to stop the other team from scoring a goal by stealing the ball or by blocking a shot.

Players dribble (bounce) the ball with one hand at a time to move in the court. They also pass the ball from one player to another during the game. The player who is in possession of the ball must pass the ball or shoot it once he has stopped dribbling. The ball is given to the other team once a shot (or a basket) has been made.

Goals and win

A goal (or a throw which results in the ball passing through the opponent's basket) gives two points to the team who makes the goal. Three points are awarded for a field goal made from outside the three-point line (or the arc). One point is awarded for a free throw won by the player of a team. A free throw is awarded when a player is fouled against by the player of the opposing team. At the end of the game, the team with the most points wins.

A slam dunk is a type of goal which occurs when a player jumps towards the basket with the ball in his hands and throws the ball through the basket while still in air. It is a very popular shot with basketball fans.

Astonishing fact

The slam dunk (a type of basketball shot) was made illegal in 1967. It was reintroduced in 1976.

Duration

Basketball games are timed. Generally speaking, basketball is either played in four quarters or two halves. The length of the quarter or half varies with the organization and is determined by said organization's governing body.

Under the FIBA (International Basketball Federation), games are played in four parts of 10 minutes. NBA (National Basketball Association), on the other hand, divides the game in four parts of 12 minutes. College games have two halves of 20 minutes each, whereas high school varsity games use 8 minute quarters.

A 15 minute half-time break is allowed under FIBA, NBA, and NCAA and a 10-minute break in high school. 5 minutes are allotted for overtime. For high school matches the overtime period is four minutes.

Only the actual playing time is recorded; the clock is stopped while the play is not active. Thus, games usually last much longer than the allotted game time, typically about two hours. After the end of each playing period the teams exchange courts.

Time-out

A coach can request for a short meeting with the players for discussing the strategy of the game for a specific number of times. These are called **time-outs**. Time-outs generally do not last more than one minute. However, NBA allows mandatory time-outs of 100 seconds. A timeout in a basketball game serves many purposes. It primarily gives your team a chance to catch their breath, gain focus and listen to the coach's instructions.

Astonishing fact

Michael Redd, an American basketball player, made 8 shots in one quarter of the game on 20 February, 2002, the most shots by any player!

Rules

Original rules

Dr James Naismith had drafted the rules for the game he invented. The basic rules of the game have not changed much since then even though other necessary changes and additions are made by authorities as required. Take a look at the original rules of the game as published by Dr. James Naismith:

1. The players can throw the ball in any direction with one or both hands.
2. The ball maybe hit in any direction with one or both hands.
3. A player can't run with the ball. The player must throw it from the spot on which he catches it.
4. The arms or the body must not be used for holding the ball.
5. A player should not hit, hold, strike, push or trip the other players with his shoulders or in other way. If he does so it will be counted as a foul. Second foul shall disqualify him until the next basket is made or, if there was evident intent to injure the person, for the whole of the game. No substitution shall be allowed.
6. A foul is striking at the ball with the fist, violation of rules three and four and such described in rule five
7. If either side makes three fouls without the opponents in the mean time making a foul, it shall count as a goal for the opponents.

8. A goal shall be made when the ball is thrown or hit from the grounds into the basket and it stays there (without falling). If the ball rests on the edges, and the opponent moves the basket, it shall count as a goal.

9. When the ball goes out of bounds, it shall be thrown back into the field and played by the first person touching it. In case of a conflict the umpire shall throw it straight into the field. The player who gets the possession of the ball is allowed five seconds. If he holds it longer, it shall go to the opponent. If any side continues to delay the game, the umpire shall call a foul on that side.

10. The umpire shall judge the behaviour of the players and shall note the fouls and notify the referee when three consecutive fouls have been made. He shall have power to disqualify people according to Rule 5.

11. The referee shall be the judge of the ball and shall decide when the ball is in play, to which side it belongs and shall keep the time. He shall decide when a goal has been made and keep account of the baskets, with any other duties that are usually performed by a scorekeeper.

12. The time shall be two fifteen-minute halves with five minutes rest between.

13. The side making the most points in that time, is declared the winner.

Since these are the old rules, all of these are not followed completely. For example, the rule regarding the duration of the game has been modified (see **Duration**). However, most of them have stayed the same and are still followed.

Astonishing fact

Rasheed Wallace, an American basketball player, once threw his sweaty jersey at one of the Piston staff in a fit of anger!!

Rules now

The most recent international rules of basketball were published on April 26, 2008 by FIBA and came into effect on October 1 of the same year.

At present, there are eight rules consisting of 50 articles, regarding equipment and facilities, team regulations, players, captains and coaches, playing regulations, violations, fouls and their penalties, special situations and the officials.

Fouls and penalties

Fouling happens by touching a player in possession of the ball with the hands or unfairly blocking a shot. Running with the ball is not allowed. The player holding the ball cannot take more than one step while holding the ball. He must continuously dribble (that is, hit the ball on the ground with the palm of his either hands) the ball. If he stops dribbling, he must pass the ball to another player or throw it at the basket. If he dribbles the ball again, he will be penalized for double dribbling.

Basketball is a non-contact game which means the players should try their best not to make contact with each other. Any sort of contact such as hitting, holding, striking, pushing or tripping, which obstructs the path of the player who has the possession of the ball, will be charged with a personal foul. Although, contact which gives no one an unfair advantage can happen. Any number of fouls may be called against a team. Every basketball foul that is committed has a specific consequence or punishment for the player and team committing the foul.

Astonishing fact

In a game between Kansas and Oklahoma on February 23, 2009, a total of 60 fouls were scored, the maximum number of fouls ever scored in the game!

When the referee declares a foul on a defensive player, the offensive player is awarded a free-throw (a shot made from the free throw line during which other players are not allowed to interfere). If the foul is committed by the offense, the ball is given to the defence.

If a player throws the ball outside the court the ball will be turned over to the opposite team. The ball is considered out of the court if it comes in contact with, or crosses over a boundary line or touches a player who is outside the court.

Unless the ball has no chance of entering the basket, no player is allowed to touch the ball while the ball is in the air moving downwards to the basket. Also, no player is allowed to touch the ball while it is on or in the basket.

If a defensive player touches it through the basket (known as basket interference) the basket is awarded to the offending team and the offending team gets the ball. If a player of the offending team touches the ball through the basket, the basket is cancelled and the defensive team is given possession of the ball.

17

Time violations

24-second limit: According to the NBA rules, the team in possession of the ball must throw the ball at the basket within 24 seconds of taking possession of the ball otherwise the opposite team is awarded the ball.

The 24-second clock is started each time a basket is made or the ball hits the rim. It also starts over if the opposing team kicks the ball. In college, teams are given 35 seconds.

10-second violation: A team must cross half of the court, that is, cross the midcourt line with the ball within 10 seconds of taking possession of the ball. Failing to do so will result in the opposite team being awarded the possession of the ball.

5-second possession violation: If a player doesn't take the ball forward within five seconds of possession of the ball, the opposing team is awarded the possession of the ball.

5-second in-bound violation: If a player is unable to pass the ball to a player in the court within 5 seconds of taking possession of the ball from out of bounds (out of the court), the opposing team is awarded the possession of the ball.

3-second rule: If an offensive player remains in the free throw lane for more than three seconds, the opposing team is awarded the possession of the ball.

Referees and umpires

The game is supervised and regulated by the referee (called the crew chief in the NBA), one or two umpires (called referee in the NBA) and the table officials. For basketball matches at college level, under the NBA, and many high schools, there are three referees on the court. The table officials keep track of each team's scores, time-violations, personal and team fouls, player substitutions, etc.

Players' positions

Each player in a basketball team is designated a specific position on the court. These positions are divided on the basis of **frontcourt** and **backcourt**. Frontcourt is the area between the midcourt line and the endline which is closest to the offence side's (the team currently in possession of the ball) basket. Backcourt is the area from the midcourt line to the endline which is furthest from offence side's basket.

Backcourt

The players who hold position in the backcourt are called **guards**. There are two guards: point guard and the shooting guard.

Point guard: The point guard is the team leader who starts the offence and controls the speed of the game. He is usually the best ball handler of the team. His job is to increase his team's efficiency. He is also known as the '1'.

Shooting guard: The shooting guard is usually the team's best shooter. A good shooting guard should be able to hit 6 m jump shots. The shooting guard can also be the team captain as well. The shooting guard needs to be able to take long-shots around the three-point line. This is because there will be much tighter defence inside the key. The shooting guard is also called the '2'.

Frontcourt

The players who hold position in the frontcourt are called **forwards** and **centres**. There are two forwards— small forward and power forward and one centre.

Small forward: Small forwards are usually shorter, quicker, and leaner than the power forwards and centres. The small forwards are expected to be an all-rounder in the game. The small forward and shooting guard positions are often interchangeable Accurate foul shooting is thus very important skill for the small forwards. The small forward is also known as the '3'.

Power forward: The power forward plays in the area that is outside of the free throw lane but is closest to the basket (also called the low post area). During offense, he can manage mid-range jump shots. During defence, he plays under the basket or against the opposing power forward. He is also called the '4' position.

Centre: Centres are usually positioned around the baseline, close to the basket. The tallest player is most likely to be given the position of centre, with typical NBA centres being about 2.13 m in height.

Centres contribute to the team by using their height and skill to score close to the basket. The centre is also called the '5' or the 'pivot'.

Scoring

Points are scored by throwing the ball into the opponent's basket. A maximum of three points are awarded to the players. Different points are awarded to players based on their location on the court and the time of the shot. Scores are awarded in the following way:

3 points: Successful shots which are made from behind the three point line are awarded 3 points.

2 points: Successful shots made from anywhere inside the three point line earn 2 points for the team.

1 point: The player who is fouled against by a player of the opposite team is awarded a free throw (or a foul shot). Every successful free throw is awarded one point.

Astonishing fact

In 1986, the three-point field goal was introduced for the first time with the three-point line set at 5.7912 m 9 inches from the centre of the basket.

Governing bodies

The International Basketball Federation (FIBA) is the highest governing authority of the basketball game. It was founded in Geneva in 1932. Argentina, Czechoslovakia, Greece, Italy, Latvia, Portugal, Romania and Switzerland were its founding member nations. The Federation declared James Naismith, (died 1939) the founder of basketball, as its Honorary President during the 1936 Summer Olympics held in Berlin.

It has now 214 members organized into five zones of Africa, Americas, Asia, Europe, and Oceania.

FIBA makes the international rules regarding the game, the equipment and the facility required, regulates the transfer of athletes across countries, and controls the appointment of international referees.

Astonishing fact

FIBA was originally known as the Fédération Internationale de Basketball Amateur (French). In 1989 it dropped the 'Amateur' from its official name but retained the 'A', as the first two letters of the word 'basketball' are also 'ba'

Major events

FIBA world championship

The FIBA World Championship is a world basketball tournament for men's national teams held once in four years since 1950 by the FIBA. A world championship for women has also been organised since 1953. Both events are now held every four years, alternating with the Olympics.

The winning team receives the Naismith Trophy, named in honour of the game's creator James Naismith. The trophy was first awarded in 1967 in Montevideo, Uruguay.

Recently, FIBA has announced three new tournaments: two 12-team, under-17 World Championships (one each for men and women) that will be played in July 2010, and an 8-team FIBA World Club Championship to be launched in October 2010.

Other basketball games

Half-court

Basketball is often played in a half-court setting since it can be difficult to reserve a full court and to have all the ten players every time one plays. This variation of the game is usually played in busy places like public gymnasiums or health clubs. In half-court games, only one basket is used.

Twenty-one

Twenty-one can be played with two or more players. There are no teams at any time in the game; each player has his or her own score. The game begins with one of the players 'breaking', or trying to shoot one free throw to determine if he or she starts the game. Players can try to stop the player with the ball from scoring a goal. The player who misses the last shot is usually responsible for defending against the offensive player. The player with the ball may throw at any time, and may collect his own rebound and shoot again. The first player to reach the score of 21 points is the winner. The game is always played on a half court.

5-3-1

5-3-1 is a variation of 21. The game starts from a shot from the free throw line. If the player who made the free shot sinks the ball in the basket he earns 5 points. He then takes the rebound from that shot, regardless of whether the ball goes in or not. He must stay at the spot that from where he grabs the rebound. Then a second shot is attempted by the player and if he makes a basket then he gets 3 points. Finally, a third shot is made by the same player which counts for 1 point. If he is able to make all the 3 shots, he gets to throw from the start again. The first person to reach 21 points wins.

War

Basketball war makes it possible for three or more teams to participate in the same game. Two teams start the game by playing a standard basketball game. When a team scores, the losing team is replaced by the next team. The same procedure is followed with the teams on the court now

Champs

In champs each player is given 5 tries to make a basket. If a shot is made within 5 tries then each player participating must either make the shot within those tries or under. If a tie occurs then a shoot off is conducted where the first shooter is chosen via rock, paper and scissors. The champ is crowned when a person starts and finishes a round.

Basketball legends

Michael Jeffrey Jordan

Country: U.S.
Born: 17th February, 1963
Height: 6 ft 6 in
Position: Shooting guard
Played for: Chicago Bulls (1984-93, 1995-98), Washington Wizards (2001-2003)

Accomplishments:

- 6 times NBA Champion (1991, 1992, 1993, 1996, 1997, 1998)
- 5 times NBA Most Valuable Player (1988, 1991-1992, 1996, 1998)
- Chosen 14 times for the NBA All-Star team (1985-1993, 1996-1998, 2002-2003)
- 6 times NBA Finals Most Valuable Professional (1991-1993, 1996-1998)
- Chosen 10 times for the All-NBA First Team (1987-1993, 1996-1998)
- 2 times NBA Slam Dunk Contest winner (1987-1988)
- Part of NBA's 50th Anniversary All-Time Team
- ACC Men's Basketball Player of the Year (1984)
- Naismith College Player of the Year (1984)
- 2 times Gold Medal Winner in the Olympics (1984, 1992)

Michael Jordan scored 16 points in his first official game for Chicago Bulls!

Wilt Chamberlain

Country: U.S.
Born: August 21, 1936 - October 12, 1999
Height: 7 ft 1 in
Position: Centre
Played for: Harlem Globetrotters (1958-1959)
Philadelphia/San Francisco Warriors (1959-1965)
Philadelphia 76ers (1965-1968)
Los Angeles Lakers (1968-1973)

Accomplishments:

- 2 times NBA Champion (1967, 1972)
- 4 times NBA Most Valuable Player (1960, 1966-1968)
- 1 time NBA Finals Most Valuable Player (1972)
- Chosen 7 times for the All-NBA First Team (1960-1962, 1964, 1966-1968)
- 1 time NBA All-Star Game Most Valuable Player (1960)
- Part of NBA All-Star game (1960-1969, 1971-1973)
- 7 times NBA scoring champion (1960-1966)
- 11 times NBA rebounding champion (1960-1963, 1966-1969, 1971-1973)

Basketball legends

Kareem Abdul-Jabbar

Country: U.S.
Born: April 16, 1947
Height: 7 ft 2 in
Position: Centre
Played for: Milwaukee Bucks (1969-1975)
Los Angeles Lakers (1975-1989)

Accomplishments:

- 6 times NBA Champion (1971, 1980, 1982, 1985, 1987-1988)
- 6 times NBA Most Valuable Player (1972-1973, 1975, 1977-1978, 1981)
- Part of NBA All-Star game (1970-1977, 1979-1989)
- 2 times NBA Finals Most Valuable Player (1971, 1985)
- 10 times All-NBA First Team (1971-1974, 1976-1977, 1980-1981, 1984, 1986)
- NBA's 50th Anniversary All-Time Team
- 3 times NCAA Men's Basketball Champion (1967-1969)
- 3 times NCAA Basketball Tournament Most Outstanding Player (1967-1969)
- Naismith College Player of the Year (1969)
- 2 times USBWA College Player of the Year (1967-1968)

Earvin 'Magic' Johnson Jr.

Country: U.S.
Born: August 14, 1959
Height: 6 ft 9 in
Position: Point guard/Power forward
Played for: Los Angeles Lakers (1979-1991, 1996)

Accomplishments:

- 5 times NBA Champion (1980, 1982, 1985, 1987-1988)
- 3 times NBA Most Valuable Player (1987, 1989-1990)
- 12 times All-Star game (1980, 1982-1992)
- 3 times NBA Finals Most Valuable Player (1980, 1982, 1987)
- 2 times NBA All-Star Game Most Valuable Player (1990, 1992)
- NBA's 50th Anniversary All-Time Team
- NCAA Men's Basketball Champion (1979)

Larry Bird

Country: U.S.
Born: December 7, 1956
Height: 6 ft 9 in
Position: Forward
Played for: Boston Celtics (1979-1992)

Accomplishments:

- 3 times NBA Champion (1981, 1984, 1986)
- 3 times NBA Most Valuable Player (1984-1986)
- 12 times All-Star (1980-1988, 1990-1992)
- 2 times NBA Finals Most Valuable Player (1984, 1986)
- 1 times NBA Coach of the Year (1998)
- 9 times All-NBA First Team Selection (1980-1988)
- 1980 NBA Rookie of the Year
- 1 times NBA All-Star Game Most Valuable Player (1982)
- 3 times NBA Three-Point Shootout Winner (1986-1988)
- NBA's 50th Anniversary All-Time Team
- 1979 USBWA College Player of the Year

Bill Russell

Country: U.S.
Born: February 12, 1934
Height: 6ft 9in
Position: Centre
Played for: Boston Celtics (1956-1969)

Accomplishments:

- 11 times NBA Champion (1957, 1959, 1960, 1961, 1962, 1963, 1964, 1965, 1966, 1968, 1969)
- 5 times NBA Most Valuable Player (1958, 1961-1963, 1965)
- 12 times NBA All-Star game (1958-1969)
- 1 times NBA All-Star Game Most Valuable Player (1963)
- NBA's 50th Anniversary All-Time Team
- NBA 35th Anniversary Team
- NBA 25th Anniversary Team
- Olympic Gold medal, Men's basketball, 1956, Melbourne

Basketball legends

Kobe Bryant

Country:	U.S.
Born:	August 23, 1978
Height:	6 ft 6 in
Position:	Shooting guard
Played for:	Los Angeles Lakers (1996-present)

Accomplishments:

- 5 times NBA Champion (2000, 2001, 2002, 2009, 2010)
- 2 times NBA Finals Most Valuable Player (2009-2010)
- NBA Most Valuable Player (2008)
- 12 times NBA All-Star (1998, 2000-2010)
- 2 times NBA scoring champion (2006-2007)
- 3 times NBA All-Star Game Most Valuable Player (2002, 2007, 2009)
- NBA Slam Dunk Contest winner (1997)
- Naismith Prep Player of the Year (1996)

Timothy 'Tim' Theodore Duncan

Country:	U.S
Born:	April 25, 1976
Height:	6 ft 11 in
Position:	Power forward/Centre
Played for:	San Antonio Spurs

Accomplishments:

- 4 times NBA Champion (1999, 2003, 2005, 2007)
- 3 times NBA Finals Most Valuable Player (1999, 2003, 2005)
- 2 times NBA Most Valuable Player (2002-2003)
- 12 times NBA All-Star (1998, 2000-2010)
- NBA All-Star Game Most Valuable Player (2000)
- USBWA College Player of the Year (1997)
- Naismith College Player of the Year (1997)
- John Wooden Award (1997)
- 2 times ACC Player of the Year (1996-1997)

Shaquille O'Neal

Country:	U.S
Born:	March 6, 1972
Height:	7 ft 1 in
Position:	Centre
Played for:	Orlando Magic (1992-1996), Los Angeles Lakers (1996-2004), Miami Heat (2004-2008), Phoenix Suns (2008-2009), Cleveland Cavaliers (2009-2010), Boston Celtics (2010-present)

Accomplishments:

- 4 times NBA Champion (2000, 2001, 2002, 2006)
- 3 times NBA Finals Most Valuable Player (2000-2002)
- NBA Most Valuable Player (2000)
- 15 times NBA All-Star (1993-1998, 2000-2007, 2009)
- 2 times NBA scoring champion (1995, 2000)
- 3 times NBA All-Star Game Most Valuable Player (2000, 2004, 2009)
- 1994 FIBA World Championship Most Valuable Player
- World championship, Canada, 1994
- Olympic gold medal, men's basketball team, Atlanta 1996

Chamique Holdsclaw

Country:	U.S
Born:	August 9, 1977
Height:	6 ft 2 in
Position:	forward
Played for:	Washington Mystics (1999–2004) Los Angeles Sparks (2005–2007) Atlanta Dream (2009) San Antonio Silver Stars (2010–present)

Accomplishments:

- Sullivan Award (1998)
- Naismith Award (1998, 1999)
- WNBA Rookie of the Year (1999)
- 6 times part of the WNBA All-Star game
- Olympic gold medal, Sydney 2000

Basketball legends

Julius Erving

Country: U.S
Born: February 22, 1950
Height: 6 ft 7 in
Position: Small forward
Played for: Virginia Squires (1971-1973)
New York Nets (1973-1976)
Philadelphia 76ers (1976-1987)

Accomplishments:

- 1 times NBA Champion (1983)
- 1 times NBA Most Valuable Player (1981)
- 11 times NBA All-Star (1977-1987)
- 2 times NBA All-Star Game Most Valuable Player (1977, 1983)
- 1 times J. Walter Kennedy Citizenship Award (1983)
- NBA's 50th Anniversary All-Time Team
- NBA 35th Anniversary Team
- 2 times ABA Champion (1974, 1976)
- 3 times ABA Most Valuable Player (1974-1976)
- 5 times ABA All-Star (1972-1976)
- 2 times ABA Playoffs Most Valuable Player (1974, 1976)

Oscar Robertson

Country: U.S
Born: November 24, 1938
Height: 6 ft 5 in
Position: point guard/ shooting guard
Played for: Cincinnati Royals (1960–1970)
Milwaukee Bucks (1970–1974)

Accomplishments:

- 1 time NBA Champion (1971)
- 1 time NBA MVP (1964)
- 12 times NBA All-Star (1961–1972)
- 9 times All-NBA First Team Selection (1961–1969)
- 2 times All-NBA Second Team Selection (1970–1971)
- 1961 NBA Rookie of the Year
- 3 times NBA All-Star Game MVP (1961, 1964, 1969)
- NBA's 50th Anniversary All-Time Team
- 2 times USBWA College Player of the Year (1959, 1960)

Lisa Leslie-Lockwood

Country: U.S.
Born: July 7, 1972
Height: 6 ft 5 in
Position: Centre
Played for: Los Angeles Sparks (1997-2009)

Accomplishments:

- 4 times Olympic gold medallist (1996, 2000, 2004, 2008)
- 2 times WNBA Champion (2001, 2002)
- 3 times WNBA Most Valuable Player (2001, 2004, 2006)
- 8 times WNBA All-Star (1999-2003, 2005, 2006, 2009)
- First player to dunk in a WNBA game
- First WNBA player to reach the 6,000 points

Diana Taurasi

Country: U.S
Born: June 11, 1982
Height: 6 ft 0 in
Position: Shooting Guard/Small Forward
Played for: Phoenix Mercury (since 2004)
Fenerbahçe (since 2010)

Accomplishments:

- Big East Player of the Year (2003, 2004)
- Wade Trophy Winner ,2003
- Naismith Award (2003, 2004)
- Nancy Lieberman Award (2003, 2004)
- NCAA National Championship (2002,2003,2004)
- NCAA Tournament MVP (2003, 2004)
- WNBA All-Star (2005, 2006, 2007, 2009)
- WNBA Championship (2007, 2009)
- WNBA Most Valuable Player (2009)
- WNBA Finals MVP (2009)
- Olympic gold medal: 2004 Athens, 2008 Beijing
- World Championship: Bronze, 2006
- U18 and U19: Gold, 2000, U18, Bronze, 2001, U19

Test Your MEMORY

1. Who invented basketball and when?
2. What is the height of the basketball hoop from the surface of the court?
3. What is the length and the width of the basketball court in an NBA match?
4. What does NBA stand for?
5. How many points are awarded for a goal made from the outside of the three-point line?
6. What is the circumference of a basketball?
7. How many players are there in a basketball team?
8. When did the first college basketball game take place?
9. How many rules were there in the rules originally published by Dr James Naismith?
10. What are the two guard positions in a basketball match?
11. Name the three frontcourt positions.
12. What does FIBA stand for?

Index

B

backboard 4, 9, 10
backcourt 19
basketball 3, 4, 5, 6, 7, 9, 10, 11, 12, 13, 15, 16, 18, 19, 21, 22, 23, 26, 28

C

centres 19
centre toss 7, 11
clock 10, 13, 18
coach 11, 13
court 3, 4, 5, 6, 7, 9, 11, 12, 17, 18, 19, 20
champs 23

D

defence 12, 17, 19
dribble 11, 12, 16

E

endlines 6

F

FIBA 5, 13, 16, 21, 22, 28
forwards 19
foul 10, 11, 14, 15, 16, 17, 19, 20

free throw 7, 8, 12, 17, 18, 19, 20
Free throw lane 8
frontcourt 19

G

goals 11
guards 7, 19

H

hoop 3, 4, 7, 9, 10
half-court 23

J

James Naismith 3, 14, 21, 22

M

midcourt line 6, 18, 19

O

offence 12, 19

P

Perimeter 8
point guard 19, 29
power forward 19

R

referee 7, 11, 15, 17, 18, 21

Rules 14, 15, 16, 17

S

shooting guard 19, 29
sidelines 6
slam dunk 12
small forward 19
substitutes 11

T

Three-point line 6
time-outs 11, 13
twenty-one 23

W

war 23